THE ABCs OF REAL ESTATE SUCCESS

by

Odest Riley, Jr

Published in Addison, TX
by Jones Co Consulting Group.

15305 Dallas Parkway, Ste 300

Addison, TX 75001

www.JonescoConsultingGroup.com

ISBN: 978-1070891231

Presented to:

_____

By:

_____

On:

_____

FOREWORD

In Real Estate, attracting success is so much more than simply having the ability to make money, help clients, and buy or sell homes. It is a mindset that involves seeing people as more than a means to financial wealth, but as a beautiful journey that allows you to meet and share life in a major life experience that impacts individual lives, families and communities.

This is a principle that Odest Riley, Jr. understands very well. He reminds us in this vibrant little book that attracting success is a way of life! Every broker, sales manager and coach should have a copy on their bookshelf to share with their agents.

We all desire success – no matter your personal definition of it. In this book, Odest shares his wisdom and strategies that help real estate professionals get out of their own way, so that they can be successful. One of the things I see in this profession over and over again, is that – more than technique and sales strategy, it's mindset that plays a key role in becoming a Top Producing Agent or Broker, and Odest has a clear understanding of this.

As I read through the wisdom in this book, I was struck by the fact that the things he focuses on can be applied not only in the real estate world but in work and life in general.

I personally feel confident enough to say if you read this book and diligently apply the principles given you will discover a new way of looking at the world and business in general, and that success is really waiting at your doorstep depending on how you view it.

Tracee Jones

CEO of The National Commercial Real Estate Association
Founder of Qualified Agent

Becoming a Lightning Rod of Success

Attracting success is the key to becoming a top producer in any field — whether it's attracting the right clients or the right team members to help you on your road to wealth.

Success can be your reality and the true purpose of this book is to give you some practical information that can help you do that. I want to help you attract your dreams so that they become your reality.

When we are honest with ourselves and live a life that is transparent it sets the stage, allowing the universe to flow through us. We become its conduit, attracting others who could benefit from the joy and skill we have to offer.

It is easy to get a license and learn how to read a contract. However, learning to read other people is a skill very few professionals, real estate or other, possess.

We work on systems, mentors, and referral groups to bring us the clients, but spend very little time working on the true skill that makes all the difference in the world.... attracting and nurturing those new relationships, which create endless opportunities for immediate client referrals and generational relationships that will sustain our business well into the future.

Television and seminars have many believing if they just automate their systems and use social media they can enjoy the spoils while autopilot takes care of all the work.

Well, I am here to challenge you to get back to the basics. The foundations of the business – relationships with individuals, teams, corporations, communities and everything in-between.

The principles expressed in this book relate specifically to the creation of attracting and nurturing the clients you want to work with.

Odest Riley, Jr.
Real Estate Expert | Author | Financier

The
ABCs

ATTITUDE

Your attitude will be a key factor in determining what direction your real estate career goes in; your life, for that matter. It will determine the altitude you rise to and the abundance you create for you and your family.

The right mental attitude will guide you through the ups and downs of a career that can be amazing at the best of times and downright ruthless at the worst times.

Keep a positive attitude and you'll be around when others have given up.

Business

I cannot express it plainly enough. Be about *your* business! Have a plan that breaks it down simply. Look for ways to incorporate it into your everyday routines.

If it does not fit, change your day or change your business. It's really that simple.

Write a business plan and stick to it even when things are not going well. It will be your guiding light in dark times.

Remember you are now a business owner and you have to be consistent in your actions if you truly want to succeed in your business. Stay focused on your craft and your plan and you will see longevity in your business.

CREATIVITY

Creativity is the key to closing deals. There are Realtors out there who will give up on clients and listings because the scenario is just too complicated for them.

By studying your craft, excelling in marketing and working with experienced lenders you can be sure you are knowledgeable enough to be creative where others are unable.

Understanding creative financing can turn that uncloseable $300,000 buyer with a 580 FICO into the owner of a new duplex in an up and coming neighborhood. It just takes the knowledge to know that is an option and resources to get it done.

DETERMINATION

Pure determination is what you will need in your journey. You must be determined to be dedicated, and be consistent in your dedication.

Determination shows up when you are dedicated in your follow-ups, cold calling, networking, and standards of service.

Dedication comes into play when you're on Day 25 and your prospects are not looking good. Yet still, you rise up on Day 26 with the same enthusiasm and focus you had on Day 1.

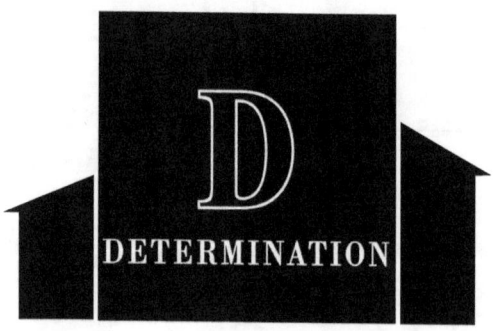

DETERMINATION

EXPERTISE

Becoming an expert will give you an edge. A lot of people know the market but, they do not know THEIR market. Be sure that you are not only educating yourself and staff on the Real Estate Market at large, but the local area in which you are located.

Be an expert on everything in your farming area – from the rank of the school system to the best restaurants and average make-up of the homes in your area. Build a reputation for service of excellence for you and your team.

FINANCE

Knowing what it takes to get a home financed will save you so much time and energy along the way.

This can be accomplished in a combination of ways. You can invest in learning how to do this yourself and/or work on building a relationship with the right financiers to ensure that you and your team have access to the highest level of financial advice and options for your clients.

I recommend a combination. You always want to make sure your team possesses basic financial knowledge. But know your experts, build those relationships as well.

No one knows everything. A wise person becomes an expert in their field and networks with other experts in complimenting fields. Networking builds relationships. Relationships are a major currency in all markets.

GRATITUDE

Gratitude has become rare. I like to remind myself as well as my team, that we work in a wonderful industry. We provide a service that provides families not only an opportunity to create financial wealth for generations (if planned right), but also to create memories that will last for generations to come.

> *Sow gratitude to reap the longevity of a fruitful career.*

Remember there are very few careers that allow you the opportunity to provide such a service to the community while producing wealth for oneself. Sadly, most service jobs pay at the lower scale in the market.

Habits

Form great habits early. Perhaps you are new so you are not even sure what those habits might be. Seek guidance from those in your craft that have achieved the success you desire and ask them.

Habits are an essential tool for any successful person. They allow you to cut down on all the unnecessary actions that do not produce the results you desire.

By forming great habits early you place yourself in a position to not change directions aimlessly. Habits birth consistency, which in turn gives you a foundation. The quality of your foundation directly affects the freedom you experience, the longevity of your business and the quality of your reputation.

INTENTIONS

What are you setting your mind to? What is the intent behind your actions?

While follow-through is walking through the door, Intent is opening it. We must learn to use our intention harmoniously with our follow-through.

The simplest way to set our intentions is to sync our calendars. Did you schedule those follow-up calls, networking meetings and important community events for the season? Have you selected which conferences you and your team will attend next season?

Be intentional in every way deed and thought.

Joy

I know of only one thing people enjoy watching more than watching something done joyfully, and that is watching it done *well* with that same joy.

And you want to know a secret…

Those that do it with joy usually do it the best.

A joyful attitude is a win-win. We all have our down days but a negative spirit sucks the life out of its host and those in close proximity. Do not allow yourself to be that negative spirit. Tend to your joy. It is key for you being able to have enough to go around.

For me educating others brings me joy, therefore I invest in quality education for myself and team so we can pass quality to our clients.

Knowledge

Acquiring knowledge is a part of the process. We follow this with applying acquired knowledge.

Two pieces of knowledge I have acquired and want to share:

1. One does not acquire more knowledge until you have applied what you have already acquired.

2. Always be fine-tuning what knowledge you have acquired.

This cycle of knowledge, acquiring and applying, will allow you to consistently perform at a faster pace and higher level.

LOVE

As corny as it may sound, loving what you do and those you do it with and for, is the key to never working a day in your life.

This does not eliminate those hard days. What it does, is make them all worth it.

Take your time preparing your mind. Allow yourself to find what you truly love. Nothing is worse than having to get up every day, doing something you do not like, with people you would rather not be around; for a purpose you do not believe in. It makes the days longer and harder. Take the time early on to ensure your hard days are worth the extra stress.

Marketing

Marketing is a 24 hour, 7 days a week job for the professional. Any time you are not marketing yourself and your business, you are throwing money out the window.

Everything about your life should tell people you are in the business. Not doing so, can really hurt when you find out your good friend is buying a million dollar beach home and did not realize they could have come to you for the transaction.

Place your mark and make sure everyone knows it's there.

No.

A matter of discernment

In the game of life and in your craft, you have to learn about the Nos. You should not only know when to use them but how to recognize them and when to use which one.

In the world, we encounter 3 types of Nos.

- The nos that should be respected.
- The nos that is a point of negotiation.
- The nos that establish and represent boundaries.

Using and respecting the nos of others is essential to a life of fewer headaches. There will be times when you need to establish your no with a client that may be overstepping their boundaries; possibly showing disrespect to you or a team member. Conveying you and your company's no here is critical. And how you do it is crucial.

Other situations will call for you to discern the point of negotiation on a sale versus the lowest possible accepted offer. You do not want to insult the seller or overbid for a buyer you may be representing.

OBLIGATION

One of your obligations is to see to it that the client is protected. Being knowledgeable on the language of contracts is a lethal piece to have in your arsenal.

There are numerous ways that we can better equip ourselves and our teams to protect our clients. None are as transferable as contractual knowledge. This skill is useful in many high revenue industries.

This may seem easy enough, however, contractual language can be tricky. Definitions are important and knowing the laws for the area you are servicing can make all the difference.

In addition to assisting clients, this skill set can reduce the chance of encountering a lawsuit. A large number of real estate lawsuits are related to contracts.

We have an obligation to protect our clients.

PROMOTION

How you promote yourself and your business is a key component to your marketing strategy. The how, when, and where you promote yourself is going to create the pool in which you pull clients from and compete in.

Examine your competitors in the market and evaluate how they are promoting themselves and their business. Do any of these strategies resonate with you or your business? Can you easily incorporate some of these same strategies into what you are already doing?

What will be your memorable calling card? That one thing your clients will talk about to their friends and family that is going to generate those referrals!

QUALITY

The quality of your work will determine the quality of your clients, which will, in turn, produce the quality of your life.

You will hear many people tell you that in the beginning, you should focus on quantity over quality. Truth is, how you start your career will have a lot to do with where you end it.

The mindset should be:

- High Quality is the standard. Not high quality is extra work.
- Sow quality. Toil with integrity. Harvest a fruitful bounty.

I have a motto:

"The quality of the work you put in should directly reflect the quality of the life you desire to live."

Ratios

Everything you do should be quantifiable. While we cannot fight the reality of the ratios, we can put our clients in a position to be on the more favorable end of them. We do this by understanding and knowing how to apply these ratios to markets we serve.

No matter how you market and promote yourself you will still only close so many deals. The numbers are a part of the game. You must learn to understand and adapt the ratios of your particular market.

Do not forget to include yourself on the favorable side of those ratios from time to time as well. Professionals in our business must remind themselves to apply the same principles we teach. A successful example is the greatest form of leadership.

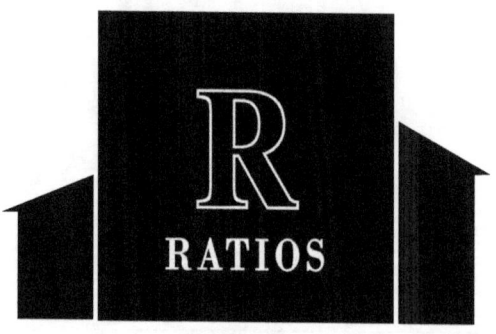

SECRET AGENT

"Hi, My Name Is… and I…" does anyone dread that statement? I challenge you to avoid at all cost becoming what I call the Secret Agent. This agent really believes they do not have to put their self out there in the actual market.

The reality is, we are in a people business and engaging with people is kind of a big part of the business. You must be dedicated to the fostering of relationships. This will require you to put yourself and your business out there.

Regardless, if it is online or offline, you must make a continuous effort to give evidence of what you do to the market you wish to serve.

TRANSACTION

Close as many transactions as you can without becoming transactional.

Once again this is a relationship business and if you only worry about closing deals for dollars, you will end up working your tail off constantly looking to find new clients.

Finding and cultivating new clients is a must, however, referral business is like residual income. Keep in mind that anyone from your kid's principal or a previous client's aunt is a potential new client. We want to attract new clients by fostering a healthy relationship in our lives period; not just in our direct market.

Understanding

Understanding and success go hand and hand. While many are knowledgeable of their market and clients few people understand them.

This is a skill that most certainly does not come overnight. It is one that is fine-tuned and the result of the application of some of those previously mentioned ABCs.

Understanding what your client wants always puts a salesperson in a good position to be successful. Understanding your client downright ensures that success continues.

One skill needed to cultivate understanding ASK(always seek knowledge) of your client.

Visuals

Appealing to the eye matters. We cannot get around this. In our market; in this business, visuals matter in this day and age it matters.

Learn enough about visuals to do the small things that make your images pop. Attention spans are getting shorter and shorter. We want to use every piece of visual capital to engage with the client and get the right message across.

Remember we are a visual species. Catching the eye and keeping the eye are two parts of the same cycle. Visuals are a key factor in both.

WALKING/WEALTH

Okay, I know it may be redundant but that should express the importance of this point. You are constantly reflecting your business, even when you are just walking down the street.

People will and are judging your business against your personal image. How you are carrying yourself in your day to day life matters. Your walk on and offline should reflect the social presence you want for you and your company.

One of our most undervalued resources is our name. Your name is your reputation and is built over years of consistently delivering on your word as an individual and company.

Your presentation of yourself can appreciate and depreciate the perception of you and your business; directly effecting your bottom line. Remember money walks and talks. Be sure you are walking and speaking a life congruent to the life of wealth you wish to attain.

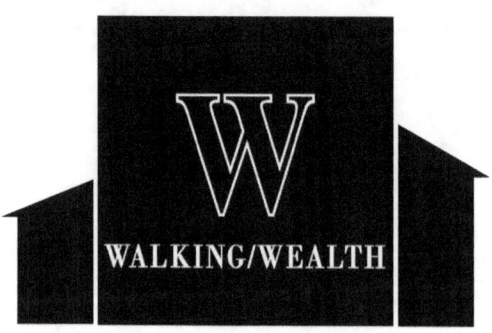

X-Factor

Another term for X-Factor would be niche. Your X-factor is your area of expertise—the one thing you specialize in your industry or field.

This service has the potential to set you apart in and of itself in your chosen field. Still, be mindful of what you select.

Consider if this X-factor has longevity or is it more of a fad. Both options will require a financial investment and commitment of time on your part. Just make sure your selection is in the best interest of you and your business.

Yo-yo

I advise my team to not become yo-yos. Believe it or not many high earning Realtors fall into this category.

You become a yo-yo when you work really hard to fill up your pipeline with clients, high earning usually, so you start making great money, but then begin to enjoy these high earnings and check out.

You take breaks too often too early causing you to always come back from these breaks jumping back into the hustle of creating a new pipeline.

Try fostering relationships at all times, even while on vacation. A 5-minute conversation over drinks in Bali can earn you more business than a 2 year back and forth with a colleague.

Nobody wants to keep starting from ground zero and quite frankly, there's no need.

ZEST + ZEAL = ZILLIONS

If you have a zest for life and a zeal for people you can become a zillionaire in this business. In the previous 25 letters, I have given you practical advice to enhance the zest in your life. Applying this advice with zeal for the people you encounter will grant you the opportunity to manage those deals that are going to add zeros and commas to your bank account.

Remaining positive, joyful, and hungry may not be easy but doing so most certainly reflects the characteristic of those with longitudinal success. Keep a smile on your face throughout your days and approach even the sourest of moments with an unmatched zeal.

After Zest + Zeal

Now that you have read the stepping stones to attracting unlimited success, understand you do not have to change your whole life in one day. Simply start by adopting one principle at a time, everyone's journey may start with a different focal point.

Take it upon yourself to go over the steps weekly, implementing as many as you can while still holding yourself to the highest standard.

Once you have become accustomed to the routines, they will become second nature. Your mind will start to create opportunities for your career that will attract the success you have always dreamed of.

Just remember, life is a privilege and as you let go of negative thoughts and open space for your success to grow, you will see simple ways to increase your success.

CREATING ENERGY

In the previous chapter, we discussed the steps to building relationships and attracting the right energy.

Energy is the key ingredient to create the success you want. By focusing on creating your energy, you attract others who are on a similar path. These new relationships give you access to more opportunities than you can create on your own.

You have duplicated yourself — a self that possesses a different set of skills than you. These relationships allow you to look into new windows.

Nurturing these types of relationships will not come cheap. They will take money, talent and time. However, the mindset must shift and see these things as an investment; not an invoice.

Most people spend too much time trying to become well rounded when they should be spending more time developing their set of unique skills and talents. Become an expert in your niche (X-Factor) and connect yourself to those who can be of benefit to and benefit from your expertise. A table of experts collaborating on a project will yield more value and profit than a room full of well-rounded individuals.

When everyone is on one accord and operating in excellence, we have a beautifully harmonized execution of our collaborative efforts.

If you are an amazing Realtor why not align yourself with a great graphic designer and salesperson? The three of you have the capacity to be ten times more successful than you will be by trying to master and do all these things on your own.

THE 10 KEYS

We are all putting out energy period! This has been proven scientifically and supported spiritually for years on end.

The question is: What type of energy are you going to put out? If an abundance of people choose to not participate in crafting their energy, this is unfortunate; and not just for them but for us as well.

I encourage each and every one of you, if you do not take away anything else from this book remember you have the power to participate in the type of energy you take in and put out. Not only that using this power is your basic human right - it is your purest expression of free will.

10 Keys focuses I have found that are reliable allies in crafting your authentic energy.

1. Silence
2. Effort
3. Inquisitiveness
4. Joy
5. Wonderment
6. Senses
7. Selfishness
8. Sleep
9. Nourishment
10. Love

1 SILENCE

This is a prescription that is often prescribed but rarely taken.

Silence is one of the hardest elements to implement and one of the most beneficial.

In the basic sense if you do not or cannot sit with your own energy who else do you expect to?

Silence is the time we discover who we truly are. Some of us, if we are honest, have parts of ourselves we never want to sit alone with. If by chance you do not like a piece of yourself, then I would like to remind you that you have the power to change it.

How do you do that?

Sit a little longer. Be silent more often. Your answers will come.

2 WONDERMENT

Children are full of wonder. They explore. They ask questions. They are never afraid to admit when someone or thing WOWs them. They are in the fullness of their moments and themselves.

Life comes along and buries us. Our schedules become more fixed and we are herded into the hustle and bustle of our daily routines and yearly cycles.

Wonderment holds space for us to be amazed.

3 INQUISITIVENESS

By now you may see that these Key Focuses overlap and aid one another in helping you to find and maintain your authentic energy.

The answers are found in the questions. This is not in the quantity of questions but of this quality. How deep are you going with your inquiries? Remember we are asking these questions of ourselves to ourselves so honesty is our best course of action.

Ask hard questions. Give honest answers and you will surely see a plan of success map out for you.

4 EFFORT

Effort is how we choose to activate our energy. This is the portion that so many fail to execute effectively and consistently.

The effort of your energy is essential to the radius in which it is able to penetrate. You have to be willing to sow into yourself so that you are producing the maximum yield.

Literally, everything affects and is affected by our energy but remember, that is also the backdrop.

The starting place is our effort to harmonize our own space within one's self. As we do that, our inner energy will radiate; affecting and attracting beyond self. The more we do this the larger that radius increases.

5 SENSES

Being in-tune with our senses is an undervalued skill. Therefore it is not taught as widely as it should be.

Syncing oneself with your body did not only help our ancestors survive in the wilderness but can help us in our concrete jungle of life.

The same energies are present simply in different forms and frequencies. We can put forth the effort to take the time to reconnect ourselves or strengthen the relationship we have with our senses.

Senses are the tiebreaker and leading role in many dealings. Just like a child, our senses pick up on clues that our logical minds may have missed.

6 SELFISHNESS

Selfishness has taken a bad wrap. By definition, selfishness is the quality or condition of being selfish. Selfish being: concerned excessively or exclusively with oneself: seeking or concentrating on one's own advantage, pleasure, or well-being without regard for others.

For our purpose – crafting and maintaining your authentic energy – we recommend you be selfish. In doing so you'd be surprised how selfless you really end up being.

Once you fully understand the concept of our collective energy you will grasp the concept and importance of crafting and maintaining your authentic energy and that this requires times, moments, maybe seasons of selfishness.

7 JOY

When you have crafted your authentic energy and are living a life that maintains it joy is a natural residual.

Remember, joy and happiness are not the same. While happiness is an expression of joy, happiness in and of itself depends on happenings.

Joy is the outcome of faith and effort. We are full of joy when we have enough faith to push through the fear and exert the efforts necessary to live out our authentic energy. For our authentic energy is the only version of us that is the right frequency to attract what we need to carry out the vision - personal and collective.

How can one not be joyous when they are living in the fullness of their gifts. Sharing thir turest self with the world. Even those hard days have a silver lining.

8 SLEEP

Sleep and silence are sisters or maybe cousins. They are in the same family but look nothing alike. Though we may experience similar benefits from them both, they are distinct as well.

Sleep is more for its physical benefits. We need this component to be consistent if we want to be able to transmit our energy and guard ourselves against unwanted energies.

An adequate amount of sleep and rest help us operate in health and excellence. Giving our bodies and minds time to recharge for reuse.

Silence is our time to connect and recharge spiritually, emotionally and maybe even mentally. Sleep is our time to do this physically.

Please note that this is just as — if not more important — than silence simply because our body is an ally in our silent times as well. Without proper sleep, all of our silent times might turn into naps instead of nourishment.

9 NOURISHMENT

Be sure you are taking time to nourish your temple and talents. Your temple, being the self, as it is where your energy is housed. Your talents as they are how you will transmit your energies to the world.

How we nourish our energy is directly linked to what kind of offering we have for ourselves, family and world.

You've heard you cannot serve from an empty cup.

Well, I'd like to expand that and say you cannot feed anyone from a bare pantry. You see the degree to which you nourish your talents and temple will determine your yield. And the yield determines your capacity to feed.

The higher your yield, the greater your capacity to feed yourself and the people that surround you.

10 LOVE

Love. Isn't that the point of it all?

We all want to feel love and be loved. I think what so many miss is that the best way to do this is to love ourselves through the process of crafting and maintaining our authentic energy.

In doing so, we not only achieve an eternal love space for ourselves but sustain an environment conducive for others to do the same.

It is a process and one that will take all of the previous 9 Key Focuses but it is well worth the investment.

This is your life to live out to its fullest capacity. Fine-tuning our energy connects us to our proper frequency. And we all want to catch that perfect wave and ride it.

Now what huh?

Well, I encourage you to start investing in creating and sustaining your authentic energy. It is of benefit to you and the rest of us.

Are you unsure of where to start? Feeling a bit overwhelmed?

We have an index of resources to help you get on track.

Or maybe you prefer hands-on assistance or one-on-one guidance?

Either way, we've got you covered.

Contact our offices today at 310-905-7421 to start discovering how you can start crafting your authentic energy now.

A SHORT STORY

Once upon a time in an urban jungle, a young man went to speak to his mentor and said, "I want to be wealthy enough so that one day I can leave this neighborhood and help take care of my family."

His mentors smiled and said, "Then do it," which caught the young man off guard, so he asked his mentor "Do what?"

His mentor replied, "The secret to wealth and freedom in this world is to find something you love and share what you love with people. This will guarantee you become successful many times over."

He explained to the boy that the more love and passion he had for his chosen field the more people would be attracted to him, all he had to do was nurture the relationships of the people he attracted and he would be wealthier than he ever imagined.

In Conclusion

The information in this book is straight forward and must be internalized by the reader for true life-changing results.

To best reap the benefits, I suggest that you read the entire book. Once you have read the book in its entirety, go back and read three to five pages daily, taking time to digest anything that is resonating to you.

Upon completion, start again. Make this a part of your daily routine and success and wealth in all their forms will be attracted to you.

About the Author

CEO & Principal of WLM Financial, a privately-held, full-service Real Estate firm. Odest specializes in consulting and advisory services for education, governmental and non-profit organizations throughout Southern California.

His practice encompasses a broad spectrum of transactional disciplines; including transaction negotiations, tenant buy-outs, relocations, lease restructure and marketing. He is an expert in strategizing market analysis, and team building.

Excelling at implementing creative solutions for difficult situations, Odest has spent the last decade providing clients with Multi-family Real Estate consultations and expertise to achieve desired goals.

Odest holds his B.A. in Public Relations and A.A. in Real Estate. He's accomplished all of this while working as an Executive Manager for a Fortune 100 Company. His passion and work ethic have given him the mindset and heart to see Real Estate as a pathway to generational wealth for his family and community. He presently holds the position of Housing Advisory Commissioner for his beloved city, Inglewood.

His achievements include:

- NLC New Leaders Council 40 under 40 Award
- Housing Advisory Commissioner – Inglewood
- Section8 Hearing Officer – Inglewood
- Minority in Real Estate Department
- Graduate – USC Ross 2015

Odest resides in Inglewood, California with his wife, Shara, and son Odest, III.

To invite Odest to speak at your event or schedule a consultation, by visiting www. OdestRiley.com